PREVAILING PRAYER

THE CHARLES G. FINNEY MEMORIAL LIBRARY

Evangelistic Sermon Series
- So Great Salvation
- The Guilt of Sin
- True and False Repentance
- God's Love for a Sinning World

Revival Sermon Series
- Victory Over the World
- True Saints
- True Submission

Sermons on Prayer
- Prevailing Prayer

PREVAILING PRAYER

SERMONS ON PRAYER

CHARLES G. FINNEY

KREGEL PUBLICATIONS
GRAND RAPIDS, MICHIGAN 49501

Prevailing Prayer, by Charles G. Finney. © 1965 by Kregel Publications, a division of Kregel, Inc. P. O. Box 2607, Grand Rapids, MI 49501. All rights reserved.

This series of sermons selected from *Sermons on the Way of Salvation* by Charles G. Finney.

Library of Congress Catalog Card No. 65-25846

ISBN   0-8254-2603-0 (pbk.)

7 8 9 10 11 Printing/Year 95 94 93 92 91

Printed in the United States of America

CONTENTS

1

PREVAILING PRAYER

"Ask, and it shall be given you. "—*Matt.* vii. 7, 8

"Ye ask and receive not, because ye ask amiss, to consume it upon your lusts. "—*James* iv. 3

I PROPOSE to consider the conditions of prevailing prayer.

The first condition is *a state of mind in which you could offer the Lord's Prayer sincerely and acceptably*.

Christ at their request taught his disciples how to pray. In doing so, he gave them an epitome of the appropriate subjects of prayer, and also threw a most important light upon the *spirit* with which all prayer should be offered. This form is exceedingly comprehensive. Every word is full of meaning. It would seem very obvious, however, that our Lord did not intend here to specify all the particular things we may pray for, but only to group together some of the great heads of subjects which are appropriate to be sought of God in prayer, and also to show us with what temper and spirit we should come before the Lord.

This is evidently not designed as a mere form, to be used always and without variation. It cannot be that Christ intended we should evermore use these

5

words in prayer, and no other words; for he never again used these precise words himself,—so far as we know from the sacred record,—but did often use other and very different words, as the Scriptures abundantly testify.

But this form answers a most admirable purpose if we understand it to be given us to teach us these two most important things; namely, what sort of blessings we may pray for, and in what spirit we should pray for them.

Most surely, then, we cannot hope to pray acceptably unless we can offer this prayer in its real *spirit*—our own hearts deeply sympathising with the spirit of this prayer. If we cannot pray the Lord's Prayer sincerely, we cannot offer any acceptable prayer at all.

Hence it becomes us to examine carefully the words of this recorded form of prayer. Yet be it remembered, it is not these words, as mere words, that God regards, or that we should value. Words themselves, apart from their meaning, and from their meaning *as used by us*, would neither please nor displease God. He looks on the heart.

Let us now refer to the Lord's Prayer, and to the connection in which it stands.

"When ye pray," says our Lord, "use not vain repetitions, as the heathen do : for they think that they shall be heard for their much speaking."

Hence there is no need that you continue to clamour unceasingly, "O Baal, hear us; O Baal, hear us". Those were indeed vain repetitions—just such as the heathen use. It is a most singular fact that the Roman Catholic church has fallen into the practice here condemned. Like the priests of Baal, in Elijah's time, they demand and practise everlasting repetitions of the same words, numbering their repetitions of Paternosters and Ave Marias by their beads, and estimating the merit of prayer by the quantity, and not the quality, of their prayers. The more repetitions, the greater the value. This principle, and the practice founded upon it, our Saviour most pointedly condemns.

So, many persons, not Roman Catholics or heathen, seem to lay much more stress upon the *amount* of prayer than upon its character and quality. They think if there can only be prayer enough, that is, repetitions enough of the same or similar words, the prayer will be certainly effective, and prevalent with God. No mistake can be greater. The entire word of God rebukes this view of the subject in the most pointed manner.

Yet, be it well considered, the precept "Use not vain repetitions," should by no means be construed to discourage the utmost perseverance and fervency of spirit in prayer. The passage does not forbid our renewing our requests from great earnestness of spirit. Our Lord himself did this in the garden, repeating his supplication " in the same words ". *Vain* repetitions are what is forbidden ;—not repetitions which gush from a burdened spirit.

This form of prayer invites us, first of all, to address the great God as " *Our Father who art in heaven* ". This authorises us to come as children and address the Most High, feeling that he is a *Father to us.*

The first petition follows, *"Hallowed be thy name"*. What is the exact idea of this language? To hallow is to sanctify; to deem and render *sacred*.

There is a passage in Peter's Epistle which may throw light on this.

He says, "Sanctify the Lord God in your hearts." The meaning seems plainly to be this: Set apart the Lord God in your hearts as the only true object of supreme, eternal adoration, worship, and praise. Place him alone on the throne of your hearts. Let him be the only hallowed object there.

So here, in the first petition of the Lord's Prayer, we pray that both ourselves and all intelligent beings may in this sense hallow the name of the Lord God and sanctify him in their hearts. Our prayer is, Let all adore thee—the infinite Father—as the only object of universal adoration, praise, worship, and love.

This prayer hence implies :—

1. A desire that this hallowing of Jehovah's name should be universal.

2. A willingness to concur heartily ourselves in this sentiment. Our own hearts are in deep sympathy with it. Our inmost souls cry out, Let God be honoured, adored, loved, worshipped, and revered by all on earth and all in heaven. Of course, praying in this spirit, we shall have the highest reverence for God. Beginning our prayer thus, it will so far be acceptable to God. Without such reverence for Jehovah's name, no prayer can possibly be acceptable. All irreverent praying is mockery, most abhorrent to the pure and exalted Jehovah.

" *Thy kingdom come*." What does this language imply ?

1. A desire that God's kingdom should be set up in the world, and all men become holy. The will is set upon this as the highest and most to be desired of all objects whatever. It becomes the supreme desire of the soul, and all other things sink into comparative insignificance before it. The mind and the judgment approve and delight in the kingdom of God as in itself infinitely excellent, and then the will harmonises most perfectly with this decision of intelligence.

Let it be well observed here that our Lord, in giving this form of prayer, assumes throughout that we shall use all this language with most profound sincerity. If any man were to use these words, and reject their spirit from his heart, his prayer would be an utter abomination before God. Whoever would pray at all, should consider that God looks on the heart, and is a *holy* God.

2. It is implied in this petition that the suppliant *does* what he can to establish this kingdom. He is actually doing all he can to promote this great end for which he prays. Else he fails entirely of evincing his sincerity. For nothing can be more sure than that every man who prays sincerely for the coming of Jehovah's kingdom, truly desires and wills that it may come ; and if so, he will neglect no means in his power to promote and hasten its coming. Hence every man who sincerely offers this petition will lay himself out to promote the object. He will seek by every means to make the truth of God universally prevalent and triumphant.

3. I might also say that the sincere offering of this

petition implies a resistance of everything inconsistent with the coming of this kingdom. This you cannot fail to understand.

We now pass to the next petition, " *Thy will be done in earth as it is in heaven*."

This petition implies that we desire to have God's will done, and that this desire is supreme.

It implies also a delight in having the will of God done by all his creatures, and a corresponding sorrow whenever it fails of being done by any intelligent being.

There is also implied a state of the will in harmony with this desire. A man whose will is averse to having his own desires granted is insincere, even although his desires are real. Such a man is not honest and consistent with himself.

In general, I remark, respecting this petition, that if it be offered sincerely, the following things must be true :—

1. The suppliant is willing that God should require all he does, and *as* he does. His heart will acquiesce both in the things required and in the manner in which God requires them. It would indeed be strange that a man should pray sincerely that God's will might be done, and yet not be willing himself that God should give law, or carry his will into effect. Such inconsistencies never can happen where the heart is truly sincere and honest before God. No, never. The honest-hearted suppliant is as willing that God's will should be done as the saints in heaven are. He delights in having it done, more than in all riches—more than in his highest earthly joy.

2. When a man offers this petition sincerely it is implied that he is really doing, himself, all the known will of God. For if he is acting contrary to his actual knowledge of God's will, it is most certain that he is not sincere in praying that God's will may be done. If he sincerely desires and is willing that God's will should be done, why does he not do it himself?

3. It implies a willingness that God should use his own discretion in the affairs of the universe, and just as really and fully in this world as in heaven itself. You all admit that in heaven God exercises a holy sovereignty. I do not mean by this, an arbitrary, unreasonable sovereignty, but I mean a control of all things according to his own infinite wisdom and love—exercising evermore his own discretion, and depending on the counsel of none but himself. Thus God reigns in heaven.

You also see that in heaven, all created beings exercise the most perfect submission and confidence in God. They all allow him to carry out his own plans, framed in wisdom and love, and they even rejoice with exceeding joy that he does. It is their highest blessedness.

Such is the state of feeling towards God universally in heaven.

And such it should be on earth. The man who offers this petition sincerely must approximate very closely to the state of mind which obtains in heaven.

He will rejoice that God appoints all things as he pleases, and that all beings should be, and do, and suffer as God ordains. If man has not such confidence in God as to be willing that he should control all events respecting his own family, his friends, all his interests,—in short for time and eternity,—then certainly his heart is not submissive to God, and it is hypocrisy for him to pray that God's will may be done on earth as in heaven. It must be hypocrisy in him, because his own heart rebels against the sentiment of his own words.

This petition offered honestly, implies nothing less than universal, unqualified submission to God. The heart really submits, and delights in its submission.

No thought is so truly pleasing as that of having God's will done evermore. A sincere offering of this prayer, or indeed of any prayer whatever, involves the fullest possible submission of all events, for time and for eternity, to the hands of God. All real prayer puts. God on the throne of the universe, and the suppliant low before him at his footstool.

4. The offering of this petition sincerely, implies. conformity of life to this state of the will. You will readily see that this must be the case, because the will governs the outward life by a law of necessity. The action of this law must be universal so long as man remains a voluntary moral agent. So long, therefore, the ultimate purpose of the will must control the outward life.

Hence the man who offers this prayer acceptably must live *as he prays*; must live according to his own prayers. It would be a strange and most unaccountable thing, indeed, if the heart should be in a state to offer this prayer sincerely, and yet should act itself out in the life directly contrary to its own expressed and supreme preference and purpose.

Such a case is impossible. The very supposition involves the absurdity of assuming that a man's supreme preference shall not control his outward life.

In saying this, however, I do not deny that a man's state of mind may change, so as to differ the next hour from what it is this. He may be in a state one hour to offer this prayer acceptably, and the next hour may act in a manner right over against his prayer.

But if in this latter hour you could know the state of his will, you would find that it is not such that he can pray acceptably, " Thy will be done ". No ; his will is so changed as to conform to what you see in his outward life.

Hence a man's state of heart may be to some extent known from his external actions. You may at least know that his heart does not sincerely offer this prayer if his life does not conform to the known will of God.

We pass to the next petition, " *Give us this day our daily bread* ".

It is plain that this implies dependence on God for all the favours and mercies we either possess or need.

The petition is remarkably comprehensive. It names only bread, and only the bread for " *this day*"; yet none can doubt that it was designed to include also our water and our needful clothing—whatever we really need for our highest health, and usefulness, and enjoyment on earth. For all these we look to God.

Our Saviour doubtless meant to give us in general the *subjects* of prayer, showing us for what things it is proper for us to pray and also the spirit with which we should pray. These are plainly the two great points which he aimed chiefly to illustrate in this remarkable form of prayer.

Whoever offers this petition sincerely, is in a state of mind to recognise and gratefully acknowledge the providence of God. He sees the hand of God in all the circumstances that affect his earthly state. The rain and the sunshine—the winds and the frosts, he sees coming, all of them, from the hand of his own Father. Hence he looks up in the spirit of a child,— saying, " Give me this day my daily bread ".

But there are those who philosophise and speculate themselves entirely out of this filial dependence on God. They arrive at such ideas of the magnitude of the universe that it becomes in their view too great for God to govern by a minute attention to particular events. Hence they see no God, other than an un-knowing Nature in the ordinary processes of vegeta-tion, or in the laws that control animal life. A certain indefinable but unintelligent power, which they call Nature, does it all. Hence they do not expect God to hear their prayers, or notice their wants. Nature will move on in its own determined channel whether they pray or restrain prayer.

Now men who hold such opinions cannot pray the Lord's Prayer without the most glaring hypocrisy. How can they offer this prayer and mean anything by it, if they truly believe that everything is nailed down to a fixed chain of events, in which no regard is had or can be had to the prayers or wants of man?

Surely, nothing is more plain than that this prayer recognises most fully the universal providence of that same infinite Father who gives us the promises, and who invites us to plead them for obtaining all the bless:ngs we can ever need.

It practically recognises God as Ruler over all.

What if a man should offer this prayer, but should add to it an appendix of this sort, " Lord, although we ask of thee our daily bread, yet thou knowest we do not believe thou hast anything at all to do with giving us each day our daily bread ; for we believe thou art too high, and thy universe too large, to admit of our supposing that thou canst attend to so small a matter as supplying our daily food. We believe that thou art so unchangeable, and the laws of nature are so fixed, that no regard can possibly be had to our prayers or our wants."

Now would this style of prayer correspond with the petitions given us by Christ, or with their obvious spirit ?

Plainly this prayer dictated by our Lord for us, implies a state of heart that leans upon God for everything—for even the most minute things that can possibly affect our happiness or be to us objects of desire. The mind looks up to the great God, expecting from him, and from him alone, every good and perfect gift. For everything we need, our eye turns naturally and spontaneously towards our great Father.

And this is a *daily* dependence. The state of mind which it implies is habitual.

We must pass now to the next petition, "*Forgive us our debts as we forgive our debtors*".

In this immediate connection, the Saviour says, "For if ye forgive men their trespasses, your Heavenly Father will also forgive you ; but if ye forgive not men their trespasses, neither will your Father forgive your trespasses". The word "trespasses" therefore, doubtless explains what is meant by debts in the Lord's Prayer. Luke, in reciting this Lord's Prayer, has it, "Forgive us our sins ; for we also forgive every one that is indebted to us". These various forms of expression serve to make the meaning quite plain. It may often happen that in such a world as this, some of my fellow-men may wrong or at least offend me—in some such way as I wrong and displease God. In such cases this petition of the Lord's Prayer implies that I forgive those who injure me, even as I pray to be forgiven myself.

The phraseology in Matthew makes the fact that we forgive others either the measure or the condition of our being forgiven ; while, as given by Luke, it seems to be at least a condition, if not a ground or reason, of the request for personal forgiveness. The former reads, "Forgive us *as* we forgive," etc., and the latter, "Forgive us, *for* we also forgive every one indebted to us".

Now on this petition I remark :—

1. It cannot possibly imply that God will forgive us our sins *while we are still committing them*. Suppose one should use this form of petition : "Lord, forgive me for having injured thee as thou knowest that I do most freely forgive all men who injure me ;" while

yet it is perfectly apparent to the man himself and to
everybody else that he is still injuring and abusing
God as much as ever. Would not such a course be
equivalent to saying, " Lord, I am very careful, thou
seest, not to injure my fellow-men, and I freely forgive
their wrongs against me ; but I care not how much I
abuse and wrong thee " ? This would be horrible !
Yet this horrible prayer is virtually invoked whenever
men ask of God forgiveness with the spirit of sin and
rebellion in their hearts.

2. This petition never reads thus, " Forgive us our
sins and *enable* us to forgive others also ". This would
be a most abominable prayer to offer to God ; certainly,
if it be understood to imply that we cannot forgive
others unless we are specially enabled to do so by
power given us in answer to prayer ; and worse still,
if this inability to forgive is imputed to God as its
Author.

However the phraseology be explained, and whatever it be understood to imply, it is common enough
in the mouths of men ; but nowhere found in the book
of God.

3. Christ, on the other hand, says, Forgive us *as*
we forgive others. We have often injured, abused, and
wronged thee. Our fellow-men have also often injured us, but thou knowest we have freely forgiven
them. Now, therefore, forgive us *as* thou seest we
have forgiven others. If thou seest that we do forgive others, then do thou indeed forgive us, and not
otherwise. We cannot ask to be ourselves forgiven on
any other condition.

4. Many seem to consider themselves quite pious if they can put up with it when they are injured or slighted ; if they can possibly control themselves so as not to break out into a passion. If, however, they are really wronged, they imagine they do well to be angry. Oh, to be sure! somebody has really wronged them, and shall they not resent it, and study how to get revenge, or, at least, redress? But mark ; the apostle Peter says, " If when ye do well and suffer for it, ye take it patiently, this is acceptable with God ". " For even hereunto were ye called," as if all Christians had received a special call to this holy example. Oh, how would such an example rebuke the spirit of the world !

5. It is one remarkable condition of being answered in prayer that we suffer ourselves to harbour no ill-will to any human being. We must forgive all that wrong us, and forgive them too *from the heart*. God as really requires us to love our enemies as to love our friends,—as really requires us to forgive others as to ask forgiveness for ourselves. Do we always bear this in mind? Are you, beloved, always careful to see to it that your state of mind towards all who may possibly have wronged you is one of real forgiveness, and do you never think of coming to God in prayer until you are sure you have a forgiving spirit yourself?

Plainly, this is one of the ways in which we may test our fitness of heart to prevail with God in prayer. "When thou standest, praying, forgive, if thou hast aught against any." Think not to gain audience before God unless thou dost most fully and heartily forgive all who may be thought to have wronged thee.

Sometimes persons of a peculiar temperament lay up grudges against others. They have enemies, against whom they not only speak evil, but know not how to speak well. Now such persons who harbour such grudges in their hearts, can no more prevail with God in prayer than the devil can. God would as soon hear the devil pray and answer his prayers as hear and answer them. They need not think to be heard;—not they!

How many times have I had occasion to rebuke this unforgiving spirit! Often, while in a place labouring to promote a revival, I have seen the workings of this jealous, unforgiving spirit, and I have felt like saying, Take these things hence! Why do you get up a prayer-meeting and think to pray to God when you know that you hate your brother; and know moreover that I know you do? Away with it! Let such professed Christians repent, break down, get into the dust at the feet of God, and men too, before they think to pray acceptably! Until they do thus repent, all their prayers are only a " smoke in the nose " before God.

Our next petition is, " *Lead us not into temptation* ". And what is implied in this?

A fear and dread of sin;—a watchfulness against temptation; an anxious solicitude lest by any means we should be overcome and fall into sin. On this point Christ often warned his disciples, and not them only, but, what he said unto them, he said unto all,— " *Watch* ".

A man not afraid of sin and temptation cannot present this petition in a manner acceptable to God.

You will observe, moreover, that this petition does not by any means imply that God leads men into temptation in order to make them sin, so that we must needs implore of him not to lead us thus, lest he should do it. No, that is not implied at all ; but the spirit of the petition is this, O Lord, thou knowest how weak I am, and how prone to sin ; therefore let thy providence guard and keep me that I may not indulge in anything whatever that may prove to me a temptation to sin.—Deliver us from all iniquity—from all the stratagems of the devil. Throw around us all thy precious guardianship, that we may be kept from sinning against thee.

How needful this protection, and how fit that we should pray for it without ceasing !

This form of prayer concludes, "*For thine is the kingdom, the power, and the glory for ever. Amen.*"

Here is an acknowledgment of the universal government of God. The suppliant recognises his supremacy and rejoices in it.

Thus it is when the mind is in the attitude of prevailing prayer. It is most perfectly natural then for us to regard the character, attributes, and kingdom of God as infinitely sacred and glorious.

How perfectly spontaneous is this feeling in the heart of all who really pray, " I ask all this because thou art a powerful, universal, and holy Sovereign. Thou art the infinite Source of all blessings. Unto thee, therefore, do I look for all needed good, either for myself or my fellow-beings " !

How deeply does the praying heart realise and rejoice in the universal supremacy of the great Jehovah !

All power, and glory, and dominion are thine, and thine only, for ever and ever. Amen and amen. Let my whole soul re-echo, Amen. Let the power and the glory be the Lord's alone for evermore. Let my soul for ever feel and utter this sentiment with its deepest and most fervent emphasis. Let God reign supreme and adored through all earth and all heaven, henceforth and for ever.

2

CONFIDENCE IN PRAYER

"Beloved, if our heart condemn us not, *then* have we confidence toward God. And whatever we ask, we receive of him, because we keep his commandments, and do those things that are pleasing in his sight."—1 *John* iii. 21, 22

IN discussing this subject, I shall,

I. SHOW THAT IF OUR HEART DOES NOT CONDEMN US, WE HAVE AND CANNOT BUT HAVE CONFIDENCE TOWARD GOD THAT HE ACCEPTS US;

II. THAT IF WE HAVE CONFIDENCE THAT OUR HEART DOES NOT CONDEMN US, WE SHALL ALSO HAVE CONFIDENCE THAT GOD WILL GRANT US WHAT WE ASK;

III. SHOW WHY THIS IS SO, AND WHY WE KNOW IT TO BE SO.

I. If our heart really does not condemn us, it is because we are conscious of being conformed to all the light we have, and of doing the whole will of God as far as we know it. While in this state it is impossible that, with right views of God's character, we should conceive of him as condemning us. Our intelligence instantly rejects the supposition that he does or can condemn us, that is, for our *present state*. We may be most deeply conscious that we have done wrong

22

heretofore, and we may feel ourselves to be most guilty
for this, and may be sure that God disapproves those
past sins of ours, and would condemn us for them even
now, if the pardoning blood of Christ had not inter-
vened ; but where pardon for past sins has been
sought and found through redeeming blood, " there is
therefore no more condemnation " for the past.   And
in reference to the present, the obvious truth is that if
our conscience fully approves of our state, and we are
conscious of having acted according to the best light
we have, it contradicts all our just ideas of God to
suppose that he condemns us.   He is a father, and
he cannot but smile on his obedient and trusting
children.

Indeed, ourselves being in this state of mind, it is
impossible for us *not* to suppose that God is well
pleased with our present state.   We cannot conceive
of him as being otherwise than pleased ; for, if he
were displeased with a state of sincere and full obedience, he would act contrary to his own character ; he
would cease to be benevolent, holy, and just.   We
cannot, therefore, conceive of him as refusing to accept
us when we are conscious of obeying his will so far as
we know it.   Suppose the case of a soul appearing
before God, fully conscious of seeking with all the
heart to please God.   In this case the soul must see
that this is such a state as must please God.

Let us turn this subject over till we get it fully before our minds.   For what is it that our conscience
rightly condemns us ?   Plainly for not obeying God
according to the best light we have.   Suppose now we

turn about and fully obey the dictates of conscience.
Then its voice approves and ceases to condemn. Now
all just views of the Deity require us to consider the
voice of conscience in both cases as only the echo of
his own. The God who condemns all disobedience
must of necessity approve of obedience; and to conceive of him as disapproving our present state would
be, in the conviction of our own minds, to condemn
him.

It is therefore by no means presumption in us to
assume that God accepts those who are conscious of
really seeking supremely to please and obey him.

Again, let it be noted that in this state with an ap-
proving conscience, we should have no self-righteousness. A man in this state would at this very moment
ascribe all his obedience to the grace of God. From
his inmost soul he would say, " By the grace of God,
I am what I am "; and nothing could be farther from
his heart than to take praise or glory to himself for
anything good. Yet I have sometimes been exceedingly astonished to hear men, and even ministers of the
gospel, speak with surprise and incredulity of such a
state as our text presupposes—a state in which a
man's conscience universally approves of his moral
state.—But why be incredulous about such a state? or
why deem it a self-righteous and sinful state? A man
in this state is as far as can be from ascribing glory to
himself. No state can be farther from self-righteousness. So far is this from being a self-righteous state,
that the fact is, every other state but this is self-righteous, and this alone is exempt from that sin. Mark

how the man in this state ascribes all to the grace of God. The apostle Paul when in this state of conscious uprightness most heartily ascribes all to grace. " I laboured, "says he, " more abundantly than they all, *yet not I, but the grace of God that is in me.*"

But, observe that, while the apostle was in that state, it was impossible that he should conceive of God as displeased with his state. Paul might greatly and justly condemn himself for his past life, and might feel assured that God disapproved and had condemned Saul, the proud persecutor, though he had since par-doned Saul, the praying penitent. But the moral state of Paul the believer, of Paul, the untiring labourer for Christ, of Paul, whose whole heart and life divine grace has now moulded into his own image,—this moral state Paul's conscience approves, and his views of God com-pel him to believe that God approves.

So of the apostle John. Hear what he says :—
" Whatsoever we ask, we receive of him, *because we keep his commandments and do those things that are pleasing in his sight*". But here rises up a man to re-buke the apostle. What ! he says, did you not know that your heart is corrupt, that you never can know all its latent wickedness, that you ought never to be so presumptuous as to suppose that you " do those things that please God "? Did you not know that no mere man does ever, even by any grace received in this life, really " keep the commandments of God so as to do those things that are pleasing in his sight "? No, says John, I did not know that. " What," rejoins his re-prover, " not know that sin is mixed with all you do

and that the least sin is displeasing to God?" Indeed, replies John, I knew I was sincerely trying to please God, and verily supposed I did please him and did keep his commandments, and that it was entirely proper to say so—all to the praise of upholding, sanctifying grace.

Again, when a man prays disinterestedly, and with a heart in full and deep sympathy with God, he may and should have confidence that God hears him. When he can say in all honesty before the Lord, Now, Lord, thou knowest that through the grace of thy Spirit my soul is set on doing good to men for thy glory; I am grieved for the dishonour done to thee, so that "rivers of water run down my eyes, because men keep not thy law," then he cannot but know that his prayers are acceptable to God.

Indeed no one, having right views of God's character, can come to him in prayer in a disinterested state of mind, and feel otherwise than that God accepts such a state of mind. Now since our heart cannot condemn us when we are in a disinterested state of mind, but must condemn any other state, it follows that if our heart does not condemn us, we shall have, and cannot but have, confidence that God hears our prayers and accepts our state as pleasing in his sight.

Again, when we are conscious of sympathising with God himself, we may know that God will answer our prayers. There never was a prayer made in this state of sympathy with God, which he failed to answer. God cannot fail to answer such a prayer without denying himself. The soul, being in sympathy with God, feels as God feels ; so that for God to deny its prayers, is to deny his own feelings, and refuse to do the very thing he himself desires. Since God cannot do this, he cannot fail of hearing the prayer that is in sympathy with his own heart.

In the state we are now considering, the Christian is conscious of praying in the Spirit, and therefore must know that his prayer is accepted before God. I say, he is conscious of this fact. Do not some of you know this ? Ye who thus live and walk with God, do you not know that the Spirit of God helps your in-firmities, and makes intercession for you according to the will of God ? Are you not very conscious of these intercessions made for you, and in your very soul, as it were, with groanings that cannot be uttered ? Your heart within pants and cries out after God, and is lifted up continually before him as spontaneously as it is when your heart sings, pouring out its deep outgush-ings of praise. You know how sometimes your heart sings, though your lips move not and you utter no sound ;—yet your heart is full of music, making mel-ody to the Lord. Even so, your soul is sometimes in the mood of spontaneous prayer, and pours out its deep-felt supplications into the ears of the Lord of Hosts just as naturally as you breathe. The silent and ceaseless echoing of your heart is, Thy kingdom come —thy kingdom come ; and although you may not utter these words, and perhaps not any words at all, yet these words are a fair expression of the overflowing de-sires of your heart.

And this deep praying of the heart goes on while

the Christian is still pursuing the common vocations
of life. The man, perhaps, is behind the counter or
in his workshop driving his plane, but his heart is com-
muning or interceding with God. You may see him
behind his plow—but his heart is deeply engrossed
with his Maker;—he follows on, and only now and
then starts up from the intense working of his mind
and finds that his land is almost finished. The student has his book open to his lesson; but his deep
musings upon God, or the irrepressible longings of his
soul in prayer, consume his mental energies, and his
eye floats unconsciously over the unnoticed page. God
fills his thoughts. He is more conscious of this deep
communion with God than he is of the external world.
The team he is driving or the book he professes to
study is by no means so really and so vividly a matter
of conscious recognition to him as is his communion
of soul with his God.

In this state the soul is fully conscious of being perfectly submissive to God. Whether he uses these
words or not, his heart would always say, " Not my
will, O Lord, but thine be done ". Hence he knows
that God will grant the blessing he asks, if he can do
so without a greater evil to his kingdom than the re-
sulting good of bestowing it. We cannot but know
that the Lord delights to answer the prayers of a submissive child of his own.

Again, when the conscience sweetly and humbly approves, it seems impossible that we should feel so
ashamed and confounded before God as to think that
he cannot hear our prayer. The fact is, it is only

those whose heart condemns them, who come before
God ashamed and confounded, and who cannot expect God to answer their prayers. These persons cannot expect to feel otherwise than confounded, until the
sting of conscious guilt is taken away by repentance
and faith in a Redeemer's blood.

Yet again, the soul in this state is not afraid to come
with humble boldness to the throne, as God invites
him to do ; for he recognises God as a real and most
gracious father, and sees in Jesus a most compassion-
ate, and condescending high priest. Of course he can
look upon God only as being always ready to receive and welcome himself to his presence.

Nor is this a self-righteous state of mind. Oh, how
often have I been amazed and agonised to hear it so
represented ! But how strange is this ! Because you
are conscious of being entirely honest before God,
therefore it is maintained that you are self-righteous !
You ascribe every good thing in yourself most heartily to divine grace, but yet you are (so some say) very
self-righteous notwithstanding ! How long will it take
some people to learn what real self-righteousness is ?
Surely it does not consist in being full of the love and
Spirit of God ; nor does humility consist in being actually
so full of sin and self-condemnation that you cannot feel
otherwise than ashamed and confounded before both
God and man.

II. We are next to consider this position, namely,
*that if our heart does not condemn us, we may have
confidence that we shall receive the things we ask.*

1. This must be so, because it is his Spirit working

in us that excites these prayers. God himself prepares the heart to pray;—the Spirit of Christ leads
this Christian to the throne of grace, and keeps him
there ; then presents the objects of prayer, enkindles
desire, draws the soul into deep sympathy with
God ; and now,—all this being wrought by the
grace and Spirit of God,—will he not answer these
prayers ? Indeed he will. How can he ever fail to
answer them ?

2. It is a remarkable fact that all real prayer seems
to be summed up in the Lord's Prayer, and especially
in those two most comprehensive petitions: " Thy
kingdom come ; thy will be done on earth as it is in
heaven ". The mind in a praying frame runs right into
these two petitions, and seems to centre here continually. Many other and various things may be specified ;
but they are all only parts and branches of this one
great blessing—Let God's kingdom come, and bear
sway on earth as it does in heaven. This is the sum
of all true prayer.

Now let it be observed that God desires this result
infinitely more than we do. When, therefore, we desire it too, we are in harmony with the heart of God,
and he cannot deny us. The blessing we crave is the
very thing which, of all others, he most delights to
bestow.

3. Yet let it be noted here that God may not answer every prayer according to its letter ; but he surely
will according to its spirit. The real spirit is evermore
this, " Thy kingdom come—thy will be done " ; and
this God will assuredly answer, because he has so

abundantly promised to do this very thing in answer to prayer.

III.   Why will God certainly answer such a prayer, and how can we know that he will?

1.   The text affirms that "whatsoever we ask, we receive of him, because we keep his commandments and do those things that are pleasing in his sight". Now we might perhaps understand this to assign our obedience as the *reason* of God's giving the blessing sought in prayer. But if we should, we should greatly err. The fundamental reason always of God's bestowing blessings is his goodness—his love. Let this be never forgotten. All good flows down from the great fountain of infinite goodness. Our obedience is only the *condition* of God's bestowing it—never the fundamental reason or ground of its bestowment. It is very common for us, in rather loose and popular language, to speak of a condition as being a *cause* or fundamental reason. But on a point like the present, we ought to use language with more precision. The true meaning on this point undoubtedly is that obedience is the condition. This being fulfilled on our part, the Lord can let his infinite benevolence flow out upon us without restraint. Obedience takes away the obstacle;— then the mighty gushings of divine love break forth. Obedience removes the obstacles;—never merits or draws down the blessing.

2.   If God were to give blessings upon any other condition, it would deceive multitudes, either respecting ourselves or himself. If he were to answer our prayers, we being in a wrong state of mind, it would

deceive others very probably ; for if they did not know us well, they would presume that we were in a right state, and might be led to consider those things in us right which are in fact wrong.

Or, if they knew that we were wrong, and yet knew that God answered our prayers, what must they think of God ? They could not avoid the conclusion that he patronises wrong-doing, and lifts up the smiles of his love upon iniquity ;—and how grievous must be the influence of such conclusions !

It should be borne in mind that God has a character to maintain. His reputation is a good to himself, and he must maintain it as an indispensable means of sustaining his moral government over other creatures. It could not be benevolent for him to take a course which would peril his own reputation as a holy God and as a patron and friend of holiness and not of sin.

3. God is well pleased when we remove the obstacles out of the way of his benevolence. He is infinitely good, and lives to do good, and for no other purpose— for no other end whatever—-except to pour forth blessings upon his creatures wherever he can without peril to the well-being of other creatures under his care and love. He exists for ever in a state of entire consecration to this end. Such benevolence as this is infinitely right in God, and nothing less than this could be right for him.

Now, if it is his delight and his life to do good, how greatly must he rejoice when we remove all obstacles out of the way ! How does his heart exult when another, and yet another, opportunity is afforded him of pouring out blessings in large and rich measure! Think of it, sinner, for it applies to you! Marvellous as you may think it, and most strange as it may seem, —judged of by human rules and human examples,— yet of God it cannot fail of being always true that he delights supremely in doing you good, and only waits till you remove the obstacles;—then would his vast love break forth, and pour its ocean tides of mercy and of grace all around about you.   Go and bow before your injured Sovereign in deep submission and real peni- tence, with faith also in Jesus for pardon, and thus put this matter to a trial!   See if you do not find that his mercies are high above the heavens!   See if anything is too great for his love to do for you!

And let each Christian make a similar proof of this amazing love.   Place yourself where mercy can reach you without violating the glorious principles of Je- hovah's moral government; and then wait and see if you do not experience the most overwhelming demonstra- tions of his love!   How greatly does your Father above delight to pour out his mighty tides of blessings!   Oh, he is never so well pleased as when he finds the chan- nel open and free for these great currents of blessings to flow forth upon his dear people!

A day or two since, I received a letter from the man in whose behalf you will recollect that I requested your prayers at a late church prayer-meeting.   This letter was full of precious interest.   The writer has long been a stranger to the blessedness of the gospel; but now he writes me: " I am sure you are praying for me, for within

a week I have experienced a peace of mind that is new
to me".

I mention this now as another proof of the wonderful readiness of our Father in heaven to hear and answer prayer. Oh, what love is this! To what shall I
compare it? and how shall I give you any adequate view
of its amazing fulness and strength? Think of a vast
body of water, pent up and suspended high above our
heads, pressing and pressing at every crevice to find an
outlet where it may gush forth. Suppose the bottom
of the vast Pacific should heave and pour its ocean
tides over all the continents of the earth. This might
illustrate the vast overflowings of the love of God; how
grace and love are mounting up far and infinitely above
all the mountains of your sins. Yes; let the deep,
broad Pacific Ocean be elevated on high and there
pent up, and then conceive of its pressure. How it
would force its way and pour out its gushing floods
wherever the least channel might be opened! And
you would not need to fear that your little wants would
drain it dry! Oh, no! you would understand how
there might be enough and to spare; how it might be
said, " Open thy mouth wide and I will fill it"; how the
promises might read, Bring ye all the tithes into my
store-house, and prove me now herewith, if I will not
open you the windows of heaven, and pour you out
blessings till there be not room enough to receive
them. The great oceans of divine love are never
drained dry. Let Christians but bring in their tithes
and make ready their vessels to receive, and then,
having fulfilled the conditions, they may " stand still

and see the salvation of God". Oh, how those moun-
tain floods of mercy run over and pour themselves all
abroad till every capacity of the soul is filled! Oh, how
your little vessels will run over and run over, as in the
case of the prophet when the widow's vessels were all
full, and he cried out, Oh, hasten, hasten! "Is there
not another vessel?" Still the oil flows on—is there
not another vessel? No more, she says; all are full;
then and only then was the flowing oil stayed. How
often have I thought of this in seasons of great revival,
when Christians really get into a praying frame,
and God seems to give them everything they ask for;
until at length the prophet cries out, Is there not yet
another vessel? Oh, bring more vessels, more vessels
yet, for still the oil is flowing and still runs over;—but
ah, the church has reached the limit of her expectation
—she has provided no more vessels :—and the heavenly
current is stayed. Infinite love can bless no more; for
faith is lacking to prepare for and receive it.

CONCLUSION

1. Many persons, being told that God answers
prayer *for Christ's* sake, overlook the condition of
obedience. They have so loose an idea of prayer, and
of our relations to God in it, and of his relations to us
and to his moral government, that they think they may
be disobedient and yet prevail through Christ. How
little do they understand the whole subject! Surely
they must have quite neglected to study their Bible to
learn the truth about prayer. They might very easily
have found it there declared, "He that turneth away

his ear from hearing the law, even his prayer shall be
an abomination ". " The sacrifice of the wicked is an
abomination to the Lord." " If I regard iniquity in my
heart, the Lord will not hear me." All this surely
teaches us that if there be the least sin in my heart, the
Lord will not hear my prayer. Nothing short of entire
obedience for the time being is the condition of acceptance with God. There must be a sincere and honest
heart—else how can you look up with humble confidence and say, My Father ; else how can you use the
name of Jesus, as your prevailing Mediator ;—and else,
how can God smile upon you before all the eyes of
angels and of pure saints above !

When men come before God with their idols set up
in their hearts, and the stumbling-block of their iniquity before their face, the Lord says, " Should I be
inquired of at all by them ? " Read and see (Ezekiel
xiv. 3-5). The Lord commissions his prophet to de-
clare unto all such, " I, the Lord, will answer him that
cometh thus, *according to the multitude of his idols* ".
Such prayers God will answer by sending not a divine
fulness, but a wasting leanness ; not grace and mercy
and peace, but barrenness and cursings and death.

Do not some of you know what this is ? You have
found in your own experience that the more you pray,
the harder your heart is. And what do you suppose
the reason of this can be ? Plainly there can be no
other reason for it than this : You come up with the
stumbling-block of your iniquity before your face, and
God answers you according, not to his great mercies,
but to the multitude of your idols.

Should you not take heed how you pray?

2.   Persons never need hesitate, because of their *past sins*, to approach God with the fullest confidence. If they now repent, and are conscious of fully and honestly returning to God with all their heart, they have no reason to fear being repulsed from the footstool of mercy.

I have sometimes heard persons express great astonishment when God heard and answered their prayers, after they had been very great and vile sinners. But such astonishment indicates but little knowledge of the matchless grace and loving kindness of our God. Look at Saul of Tarsus. Once a bitter and mad persecutor, proud in his vain Pharisaism ;—but now repenting, returning, and forgiven ;—mark what power he has with God in prayer. In fact, after penitence, God pardons so fully that, as his word declares, he remembers their iniquities no more. Then the Lord places the pardoned soul on a footing where he can prevail with God as truly and as well as any angel in heaven can ! So far as the Bible gives us light on this subject, we must conclude that all this is true. And why? Not because the pardoned Christian is more righteous than an angel ; but because he is equally accepted with the purest angel, and has, besides, the merits and mediation of Jesus Christ,—all made available to him when he uses this all-prevalent name. Oh, there is a world of meaning in this so-little-thought-of arrangement for prayer *in Jesus' name !* The value of Christ's merits is all at your disposal. If Jesus Christ could obtain any blessing at the court of heaven, you may obtain the same by asking in his name—it being supposed of course that you fulfil the conditions of acceptable prayer. If you come and pray in the spirit of Christ,—his Spirit making intercession with your spirit, and your faith taking hold of his all-meritorious name,—you may have his intercessions before the throne in your behalf, and whatever Christ can obtain there, he will obtain for you. Ask, therefore, now,—so Christ himself invites and promises,—" ask and receive, that your joy may be full ".

Oh, what a vantage-ground is this upon which God has placed Christians! Oh, what a foundation on which to stand and plead with most prevailing power! How wonderful! First, God bestows pardon, takes away the sting of death ; restores peace of conscience and joy in believing : then gives the benefit of Christ's intercession ; and then invites Christians to ask what they will! Oh, how mighty, how prevalent, might every Christian become in prayer! Doubtless we may say that a church living with God, and fully meeting the conditions of acceptable prayer, might have more power with God than so many angels. And shall we hear professed Christians talk of having no power with God! Alas, alas! such surely know not their blessed birthright. They have not yet begun to know the gospel of the Son of God!

3. Many continue the forms of prayer when they are living in sin, and do not try to reform, and even have no sincere desire to reform. All such persons should know that they grievously provoke the Lord to answer their prayers with fearful judgments.

4. It is only those that live and walk with God whose prayers are of any avail to themselves, to the church, or to the world. Only those whose conscience does not condemn them, and who live in a state of conscious acceptance with God. They can pray. According to our text, they receive whatever they ask, because they keep his commandments and do the things that are pleasing in his sight.

5. When those who have been the greatest sinners will turn to God, they may prevail as really as if they had never sinned at all. When God forgives through the blood of Jesus, it is real forgiveness, and the pardoned penitent is welcomed as a child to the bosom of infinite love. For Jesus' sake God receives him without the least danger of its being inferred that himself cares not for sin. Oh, he told the universe once for all, how utterly he hated sin. He made this point known when he caused his well-beloved Son to bear our sins in his own body on the tree, and it pleased the Father to bruise him and hide his face from even the Son of his love. Oh, what a beautiful, glorious thing this gospel system is! In it God has made such manifestations of his regard for his law, that now he has nothing to fear in showing favour to any and every sinner who believes in Christ. If this believing sinner will also put away his sin; if he will only say, In the name of the Lord I put them all away—all—now—for ever; let him do this with all his heart, and God will not fear to embrace him as a son;—this penitent need fear nothing so long as he hides himself in the open cleft of this blessed Rock of ages.

3

PRAYING ALWAYS

" He spake a parable unto them to this end, that men ought always to pray, and not to faint."—*Luke* xviii. 1

IN discussing the subject of *prayer*, presented in our text, I propose to inquire,

   I. WHY MEN SHOULD PRAY AT ALL ;

   II. WHY MEN SHOULD PRAY ALWAYS AND NOT FAINT ;

   III. WHY THEY DO NOT PRAY ALWAYS.

   I. Our dependence on God is universal, extending to all things. This fact is known and acknowledged. None but atheists presume to call it in question.

Prayer is the dictate of our nature. By the voice of nature this duty is revealed as plainly as possible. We feel the pressure of our wants, and our instincts cry out to a higher power for relief in their supply. You may see this in the case of the most wicked man, as well as in the case of good men. The wicked, when in distress, cry out to God for help. Indeed mankind have given evidence of this in all ages and in every nation ;— showing both the universal necessity of prayer, and that it is a dictate of our nature to look up to a God above.

It is a primitive conviction of our minds that God does hear and answer prayer. If men did not assume this to be the case, why should they pray? The fact that men do spontaneously pray, shows that they really expect God to hear prayer. It is contrary to all our original belief to assume that events occur under some law of concatenation, too rigid for the Almighty to break, and which he never attempts to adjust according to his will. Men do not naturally believe any such thing as this.

The objection to prayer, that God is unchangeable, and therefore cannot turn aside to hear prayer, is altogether a fallacy and the result of ignorance. Consider what is the true idea of God's unchangeableness. Surely, it is not that his course of conduct never changes to meet circumstances; but it is this—that his *character* never changes; that his nature and the principles which control his voluntary action remain eternally the same. All his natural, all his moral, attributes remain for ever unchanged. This is all that can rationally be implied in God's immutability.

Now, his hearing and answering prayer imply no change of character—no change in his principles of action. Indeed, if you ask why he ever answers prayer at all, the answer must be, Because he is unchangeable. Prayer brings the suppliant into new relations to God's kingdom; and to meet these new relations, God's unchangeable principles require him to change the course of his administration. He answers prayer because he is unchangeably benevolent. It is not because his benevolence changes, but because it does *not* change, that he answers prayer. Who can suppose that God's answering prayer implies any change in his moral character? For example, if a man, in prayer, repents, God forgives; if he does not repent of present sin, God does not forgive;—and who does not see that God's immutability must require this course at his hands? Suppose God did not change his conduct when men change their character and their attitude towards him. This would imply fickleness—an utter absence of fixed principles. His unchangeable goodness must therefore imply that, when his creatures change morally, he changes his course, and conforms to their new position. Any other view of the case is simply absurd, and only the result of ignorance. Strange that men should hold it to be inconsistent for God to change, and give rain in answer to prayer, or give any needed spiritual blessings to those who ask them!

Intercourse with God is a necessity of moral beings, demanded by creatures as a necessity of their natures. No doubt this is true in heaven itself, and the fact that this want of their natures is so gloriously supplied there, makes heaven. The Bible represents spirits in heaven as praying. We hear then crying out, "How long, O Lord, holy and true, dost thou not judge and avenge our blood on them that dwell on the earth?" (Rev. vi. 10). True, their subjects of prayer are not in all respects the same as ours: we have things to pray for which they have no occasion to ask for themselves. They are neither sick nor sinful; but can you suppose they never pray, "Thy kingdom come"? Have they lost all sympathy with those interests of Zion? Far from it. Knowing more of the value of those interests, they no doubt feel more deeply their importance, and pray more earnestly for their promotion. From the nature of the case, God's treatment of the inhabitants of heaven must be conditioned on their voluntary course in regard to him and his kingdom. It must be governed and determined by their knowledge, their progress in knowledge, and their improvement of the means and powers at their command. Obviously their voluntary worship, gratitude, thanksgiving, and service of every sort, must vary their relations to God, and consequently his course towards them. He will do many things to them and for them which he could not do if they did not pray, and praise, and love, and study, and labour. This must be true, even in heaven, of apostles and prophets, and of all glorified saints. God makes to them successive revelations of himself, each successively higher than the preceding, and all dependent on their voluntary devotion to him and to his glory. They are for ever advancing in his service, full of worship, praise, adoration, and this only prepares them the more to be sent on missions of love and service, and to be employed as the interests of God's kingdom require. Hence we see that God's conduct towards saints in heaven depends on their own voluntary course and bearing towards him. This is a necessity of any and every moral system. If saints in heaven are moral agents, and God's government over them is also moral, all these results must follow. In this world sin exists ; and in this fact we see an obvious necessity for this law of moral administration. But the holy in heaven are no less moral and responsible than the sinning on earth. The great object of God's administration is to assimilate moral beings to himself; hence he must make his treatment of them depend on their moral course towards him.

In regard to saints on earth, how can God do them any good unless he can draw them to himself in prayer and praise? This is one of the most evident necessities that can be named. Men irresistibly feel the propriety of confession and supplication, in order to forgiveness. This feeling lies among the primitive affirmations of the mind. Men know that, if they would be healed of sin, they must seek and find God.

II. But why pray *so much and so often?* Why the exhortation to *pray always and not to faint?*

The case presented in the context is very strong. Whether it be history or supposition does not affect the merits of the case as given us to illustrate importunity in prayer. The poor widow persevered. She kept coming and would not be discouraged. By dint of perseverance simply, she succeeded. The judge who cared not for God or man did care somewhat for his own comfort and quiet, and therefore thought it wise to listen to her story and grant her request. Upon this case our Lord seized, to enforce and encourage importunity in prayer. Hear his argument. "Shall not God,"—who is by no means unjust, but whose compassions are a great deep,—"shall not such a God avenge his own elect, who cry day and night unto him, though he seem to bear long" in delaying to answer their prayers? "I tell you he will avenge them speedily."

1. Men ought to pray always, because they always need the influence of prayer. Consider what is implied in prayer and what prayer does for you. Prayer bathes the soul in an atmosphere of the divine presence. Prayer communes with God and brings the whole mind under the hallowed influence of such communion. Prayer goes to God to seek pardon and find mercy and grace to help. How obvious, then, that we always need its influence on our hearts and lives! Truly, we need not wonder that God should enjoin it upon us to pray always.

2. God needs prayer from us as a condition of his doing to us and for us all he would. He loves us and sees a thousand blessings that we need, and that he would delight to bestow; but yet he cannot bestow them except on condition that we ask for them in Jesus' name. His treatment of us and his bestowment of blessings upon us must depend upon our views and conduct,—whether we feel our dependence on him, whether we confess and forsake all sin, whether we trust him and thoroughly honour him in all things. His action towards us must depend upon our attitude towards him. It is essential in the management of a moral system that we should pray and trust, in order that he may freely and abundantly give, and especially that he may give in a way safe to us and honourable to himself. Nothing can be substituted for our own praying, either in its relations to God or to ourselves. We cannot get along without the personal benefit of prayer, confession, trust, and praise. You cannot substitute instruction, ever so much or so good; for these

things must enter into the soul's *experience ;* you must feel them before God, and carry out the life and power of these truths in your very heart before the Lord ; else they are worse than unknown to you. You are not likely to understand many of these things without prayer ; and even if you were to understand them, and yet not pray, the knowledge would only be a curse to you.

What can be so useful to us, sinners, as direct communion with God—the searching of the heart which it induces—the humility, the confessions, the supplications ? Other things have their use. Instruction is good ; reading God's word may be a blessing ; communion with the saints is pleasant ; but what are they all, compared with personal intercourse with God ? Nothing else can make the soul so sick of sin, and so dead to the world. Nothing else breathes such spiritual life into the soul as real prayer.

Prayer also prepares us the better to receive all blessings from God, and hence should be constant.

Prayer pleases God as governor of the universe, because it puts us in a position in which he can bless us and gratify his own benevolence.

Search the history of the world, and you will find that where there has been most true prayer, and the soul has been most deeply imbued with the divine presence, there God has most abundantly and richly blessed the soul. Who does not know that holy men of old were eminent for usefulness and power according as they were faithful and mighty in prayer ?

The more we pray, the more shall we be enlightened ;

for surely they are most enlightened who pray most.
If we go no farther in divine things than human reason
can carry us, we get little indeed from God.

The more men pray, the more they will love prayer,
and the more will they enjoy God. On the other hand,
the more we pray,—in real prayer,—the more will God
delight in us. Observe this which I say—*Delight;* the
more will God truly DELIGHT in us. This is not merely
the love of benevolence, for God is benevolent to all ;
but he delights in his praying children in the sense
of having complacency in their character. The Bible
often speaks of the great interest which God takes in
those who live near him in much prayer. This is
naturally and necessarily the case. Why should not
God delight in those who delight in him ?

The more we pray, the more God loves to manifest
to others that he delights in us, and hears our prayers.
If his children live lives of much prayer, God delights
to honour them, as an encouragement to others to
pray. They come into a position in which he can
bless them and can make his blessings on them result
in good to others—thus doubly gratifying the benevolence of his heart.

We can never reach a position in which we shall not
need prayer. Who believes that saints in heaven will
have no need of prayer ? True, they will have perfect
faith, but this, so far from precluding prayer, only the
more ensures it. Men have strangely assumed, that if
there were only perfect faith, prayer would cease.

Nothing can be more false and groundless. Certainly,
then, we never can get beyond prayer.

If I had time I should like to show how the manner of prayer varies as Christians advance in holiness. They pray not less, but more, and they know better *how* to pray. When the natural life is mingled largely with the spiritual, there is an outward effervescing, which passes away as the soul comes nearer to God. You would suppose there is less excitement, and there *is* less of animal excitement; but the deep fountains of the soul flow in unbroken sympathy with God.

We can never get beyond the point where prayer is greatly useful to us. The more the heart breathes after God, and rises towards him in heavenly aspirations, the more useful do such exercises become. The aged Christian finds himself more and more benefited in prayer as he draws more and more near to God. The more he prays, the more he sees the wisdom and necessity of prayer for his own spiritual good.

The very fact that prayer is so great a privilege to sinners makes it most honourable to God to hear prayer. Some think it disgraceful to God. What a sentiment! It assumes that God's real greatness consists in his being so high above us as to have no regard for us whatever. Not so with God. He who regards alike the flight of an archangel and the fall of a sparrow— before whose eye no possible event is too minute for his attention—no insect too small for his notice and his love,—his infinite glory is manifest in this very fact, that nothing is too lofty or too low for his regard. None are too insignificant to miss sympathy—none too mean to share his kindness.

Many talk of prayer as only a duty, not a privilege ; but with this view of it they cannot pray acceptably. When your children, full of wants, come running to you in prayer, do they come because it is a duty? No, indeed! They come because it is their privilege. They regard it as their privilege. Other children do not feel so towards you. And it *is* a wonderful privilege! Who does not know it and feel it to be so? Shall we then ever fail to avail ourselves of it ?

Finally, we are sure to prevail if we thoroughly persevere, and pray always, and do not faint. Let this suffice to induce perseverance in prayer. Do you need blessings? and yet are they delayed ? Pray always and never faint ; so shall you obtain all you need.

III. Our third general inquiry is, *Why do not men pray always ?* Many reasons exist.

1. In the case of some, because the enmity of their hearts towards God is such that they are shy, and dread prayer. They have so strong a dislike to God, they cannot make up their minds to come near to him in prayer.

2. Some are self-righteous and self-ignorant, and therefore have no heart to pray. Their self-righteousness makes them feel strong enough without prayer, and self-ignorance prevents their feeling their own real wants.

3. Unbelief keeps others from constant prayer. They have not confidence enough in God as ready to answer prayer. Of course, with such unbelief in their hearts, they will not pray always.

4. Sophistry prevents others. I have alluded to

some of its forms. They say, God, being immutable, never changes his course ; or they urge that there is no need of prayer, inasmuch as God will surely do just right, although nobody should pray. These are *little* sophistries, such as ignorant minds get up and stumble over. It is wonderful that any minds can be so ignorant and so unthinking as to be influenced by these sophistries. I can recollect how these objections to prayer came up many years since before my mind, but were instantly answered and set aside, they seemed so absurd. This, for instance,—that God had framed the universe so wisely that there is no *need* of prayer, and indeed no *room* for it. My answer was ready. What was God's object in making and arranging his universe? Was it to show himself to be a good *mechanic*, so skilful that he can make a universe to run itself, without his constant agency? Was *this* his object? *No !* But his object was to plant in this universe intelligent minds, and then reveal himself to them, and draw them to love and trust their own infinite Father. This object is every way noble and worthy of a God. But the other notion is horrible! It takes from God every endearing attribute, and leaves him only a *good mechanic !*

The idea that God mingles his agency continually in human affairs, prevails everywhere among all minds in all ages. Everywhere they have seen God revealing himself. They expect such revelations of God. They have believed in them, and have seen how essential this fact is to that confidence and love which belong to a moral government. It seems passing strange that

men can sophisticate themselves into such nonsense as
this ! Insufferable nonsense are all such objections !

On one occasion, when it had been very wet and
came off suddenly very dry, the question arose, How
can you vindicate the providence of God ? At first
the question stung me ; I stopped, considered it a few
moments, and then asked, What can his object be in
giving us weather at all ? Why does he send, or not
send, rain ? If the object be to raise as many potatoes
as possible, this is not the wisest course. But if the
object be to make us feel our dependence, this *is* the
wisest course possible. What if God were to raise
harvests enough in one year to supply us for the next
ten ? We might all become atheists. We should be
very likely to think we could live without God. But
now, every day and every year, he shuts us up to depend on himself. Who does not see that a moral
government ordered on any other system would work
ruin ?

Another reason is, men have no real sense of sin
or of any spiritual want ; no consciousness of guilt.
While in this state of mind, it need not be expected
that men will pray.

In the other extreme, after becoming deeply con-
victed, they fall into despair and think it does no good
to pray.

Another reason for not praying much is found in
self-righteous conceptions of what is requisite to success in prayer. One says, I am too degraded, and am
not good enough to pray. This objection is founded
altogether in self-righteous notions—assuming that your

own goodness must be the ground or reason for God's hearing your prayer.

A reason with many for little prayer is, their worldly-mindedness. Their minds are so filled with thoughts of a worldly nature, they cannot get into the spirit of prayer.

Again, in the case of some, their own experience discourages them. They have often prayed, yet with little success. This brings them into a sceptical attitude in regard to prayer. Very likely the real reason of their failure has been the lack of perseverance. They have not obeyed this precept which urges that men pray always, and never faint.

CONCLUSION

It is no loss of time to pray. Many think it chiefly or wholly lost time. They are so full of business, they say, and assume that prayer will spoil their business. I tell you, that your business, if it be of such sort as ought to be done at all, will go all the better for much prayer. Rise from your bed a little earlier, and pray. Get time somehow—by almost any imaginable sacrifice, sooner than forego prayer. Are you studying? It is no loss of time to pray, as I know very well by my own experience. If I am to preach, with only two hours for preparation, I give one hour to prayer. If I were to study anything—let it be Virgil or Geometry, I would by all means pray first. Prayer enlarges and illumines the mind. It is like coming into the presence of a master spirit.

4

PRAYER FOR THE HOLY SPIRIT

" If a son shall ask bread of any of you that is a father, will he give him a stone? or if he ask a fish, will he for a fish give him a serpent? or if he shall ask an egg, will he offer him a scorpion? If ye then, being evil, know how to give good gifts unto your children: how much more shall your heavenly Father give the Holy Spirit to them that ask him? "—*Luke* xi. 11-13

THESE verses form the concluding part of a very remarkable discourse of our Lord to his disciples on prayer. It was introduced by their request that he would teach them how to pray. In answer to this request, he gave them what we are wont to call the Lord's Prayer, followed by a forcible illustration of the value of importunity, which he still further applied and enforced by renewing the general promise, " Ask, and it shall be given you ". Then to confirm their faith still more, he expands the idea that God is their Father, and should be approached in prayer as if he were an infinitely kind and loving parent. This constitutes the leading idea in the strong appeal made in our text. " If a son shall ask bread of any of you that is a father, will he give him a stone? or if he ask a fish, will he for a fish give him a serpent? or if he shall ask an egg, will he give him a scorpion? If ye then, being evil, know how to give good gifts unto your children: how

much more shall your heavenly Father give the Holy
Spirit to them that ask him?"

1. Remarking upon this text, I first observe that,
when we rightly understand the matter, we shall see
that the gift of the Holy Ghost comprehends all we
need spiritually. It secures to us that union with God
which is eternal life. It implies conversion, which consists in the will's being submitted to God's control.
Sanctification is (1) this union of the will to God per-
fected and perpetuated; (2) the ascendancy of this
state of the will over the entire sensibilities, so that the
whole mind is drawn into union and sympathy with
the mind and heart of God.

2. It is supremely easy to obtain this gift from God.
In other words, it is easy to obtain from God all spiritual blessings that we truly need. If this be not so,
what shall we think of these words of Christ? How
can we by any means explain them consistently with
fair truthfulness? Surely, it is easy for children to get
really good things from their father. Which of you,
being a father, does not know it to be easy for your
children to get good things from you? You know in
your own experience that they obtain without difficulty
even from you, all the real good they need, provided it
be in your power to give it. But you are sometimes
"evil," and Christ implies that, since God is never evil,
but always infinitely good, it is much more easy for one
to get the Holy Spirit than even for your children to
get bread from your hands. "*Much more!*" What
words of meaning in such a connection as this! Every
father knows there is nothing in the way of his children

getting from him all the good things they really need and which he has to give. Every such parent values these good things for the sake of giving them to his children. For this, parents toil and plan for their children's sake. Can they then be averse or even slow to give these things to their children?

Yet God is much more ready to give his Spirit. My language, therefore, is not at all too strong. If God is much more ready and willing to give his children good things than you are to give to yours, then surely it must be easy, and not difficult, to get spiritual blessings, even to the utmost extent of our wants.

Let this argument come home to the hearts of those of you who are parents. Surely, you must feel its force. Christ must be a false teacher if this be not so. It must be that this great gift, which in itself comprehends all spiritual gifts, is most easily obtained, and in any amount which our souls need.

3. How very injurious and dishonourable to God are the practical views of almost all men on this subject! The dependence of men on the Holy Spirit has come to be the standing apology for moral and spiritual delinquency. Men everywhere profess to want the Holy Spirit, and, more or less, to feel their need, and to be praying for this gift; but continually and everywhere they complain that they do not get it. These complaints assume, both directly and indirectly, that it is very difficult to get this gift;—that God keeps his children on very low diet, and on the smallest possible amount even of that; that he deals out their spiritual bread and water in most stinted amount—as if he pur-

posed to keep his children only an inch above starvation.
Pass among the churches, and hear what they say and
how they pray ;—and what would you think?   How
would you be shocked at the strange, may I not say,
blasphemous assumptions which they make concerning
God's policy in giving, or rathèr *not* giving, the Holy
Spirit to those that ask him!   I can speak from experience and personal observation.   When I began to attend prayer-meetings, this fact to which I have alluded
struck me as very strange.   I had never attended a
prayer-meeting till I had come to manhood, for my
situation in this respect was very unlike your here.
But after I came to manhood, and prayer-meetings
were held in the place where I lived, I used to attend
them very steadily.   It was a matter of great interest
to me, more than I can explain, or well express.   I was
filled with wonder to hear Christians pray, and the
more so as I then began to read my Bible, and to find
in it such things as we have in our text to-day.   To
read such promises, and then hear Christians talk, was
surprising.   What they did say, coupled with what they
seemed to mean, would run thus : I have a duty to
perform at this meeting : I cannot go away without
doing it.   I want to testify that religion is a good
thing,—a very good thing,—although I have not got
much of it.   I believe God is a hearer of prayer, and
yet I don't think he hears mine—certainly not to much
purpose.   I believe that prayer brings to us the Holy
Spirit, and yet, though I have always been praying for
this Spirit, I have scarcely ever received it.

Such seemed to be the strain of their talking and

thinking, and I must say that it puzzled me greatly. I have reason to know that it has often puzzled others. Within a few years past, I have found this to be the standing objection of unconverted men. They say, " I cannot hold out if I should be converted—it is so difficult to get and to keep the Holy Spirit ". They appeal to professed Christians and say, Look at them : they are not engaged in religion ; they are not doing their Master's work in good earnest, and they confess it ; they have not the Spirit, and they confess it ; they bear a living testimony that these promises are of very little practical value.

Now, these are plain matters of fact, and should be deeply pondered by all professed Christians. The Christian life of multitudes is nothing less than a flat denial of the great truths of the Bible.

Often, when I am urging Christians to be filled with the Holy Ghost, I am asked, Do you really think this gift is for me ? Do you think all can have it who will ? If you tell them of instances, here and there, of persons who walk in the light, and are filled with the Spirit, they reply, Are not those very special cases ? Are they not the favoured few, enjoying a blessing that only a few can hope to enjoy ?

Here you should carefully observe, that the question is not, whether few or many have this blessing ; but, Is it practically within reach of all ? Is it indeed available to all ? Is the gift actually tendered to all in the fullest and highest sense ? Is it easy to possess it ? These being the real questions, we must see that the teachings of the text cannot be mistaken on this subject.

Either Christ testified falsely of this matter, or this gift is available to all, and is easily obtained. For, of the meaning and scope of his language, there can be no doubt. No language can be plainer. No illustrations could be more clear, and none could easily be found that are stronger.

4. How shall we account for this impression, so extensively pervading the church, that the Holy Spirit can rarely be obtained in ample, satisfying fulness, and then only with the greatest difficulty?

This impression obviously grows out of the current experience of the church. In fact, but few seem to have this conscious communion with God through the Spirit; but few seem really to walk with God and be filled with his Spirit.

When I say *few*, I must explain myself to mean few relatively to the whole number of professed Christians. Taken absolutely, the number is great and always has been. Sometimes, some have thought the number to be small, but they were mistaken. Elijah thought himself alone, but God gave him to understand that there were many—a host, spoken of as seven thousand—who had never bowed the knee to Baal. Ordinarily, such a use of the sacred number seven, is to be taken for a large, indefinite sum, much larger than if taken definitely. It may be so here. Even *then*, in that exceedingly dark age, there were yet many who stood unflinchingly for God!

It is a curious fact that persons who have really the most piety are often supposed to have the least, so few there are who judge of piety as God does. Those who preach the real gospel are often refreshed to find some in almost every congregation who manifestly embrace it. You can judge by their very looks,—their eyes shine and their faces are all aglow—almost like the face of Moses, descended from the mount.

But theirs is not the common experience of professed Christians. The common one, which has served to create the general impression as to the difficulty of obtaining the Holy Spirit, is indeed utterly unlike this. The great body of nominal Christians have not the Spirit, within the meaning of Romans viii. They cannot say, " The law of the Spirit of life in Christ Jesus hath made me free from the law of sin and death ". It is not true of them that they " walk not after the flesh, but after the Spirit ". Comparatively few of all know in their own conscious experience that they live and abide in the Spirit.

Here is another fact. Many are praying—apparently—for the Spirit of God, but do not get it. If you go to a prayer-meeting, you hear everybody pray for this gift. It is so, also, in the family, and probably in the closet also. Yet, strange to tell, they do not get it. This experience of much prayer for this blessing, and much failure to get it, is everywhere common. Churches have their prayer-meetings, years and years in succession, praying for the Spirit, but they do not get it. In view of this fact, we must conclude, either that the promise is not reliable, or that the prayer does not meet the conditions of the promise. I shall take up this alternative by-and-by ; just now, my business is to account for the prevalent impression that the Spirit of God is hard to get and keep, even in answer to prayer,—a fact which obviously is accounted for by the current experience of nominal Christians.

It should also be said that the churches have been taught that God is a sovereign, in such a sense that his gift of the spirit is only occasional, and it is then given without any connection with apparent causes— not dependent, by any means, on the fulfilment of conditions on our part. The common idea of sovereignty excludes the idea that God holds this blessing free to all, on condition of real prayer for it. I say *real* prayer, for I must show you by-and-by that much of the apparent praying of the church for the Spirit is not real prayer. It is this spurious, selfish praying that leads to so much misconception as to the bestowment of the Holy Spirit.

Some of you may remember that I have related to you my experience at one time, when my mind was greatly exercised on this promise,—how I told the Lord I could not believe it. It was contrary to my conscious experience, and I could not believe anything which contradicted my conscious experience. At that time the Lord kindly and in great mercy rebuked my unbelief, and showed me that the fault was altogether mine, and in no part his.

Multitudes pray for the Spirit as I had done, and are in like manner disappointed because they do not get it. They are not conscious of being hypocrites ; but they do not thoroughly know their own spirits. They think they are ready to make any sacrifices to obtain it. They do not seem to know that the difficulty is all with them. They fail to realise how rich and full the promise is. It all seems to them quite unaccountable that their prayer should not be answered. Often they sweat with agony of mind in their efforts to solve this mystery. They cannot bear to say that God's word is false, and they cannot see that it is true. It is apparently contradicted by their experience. This fact creates the agonising perplexity.

5. In the next place, how can we reconcile this experience with Christ's veracity? How can we explain this experience according to the facts in the case, and yet show that Christ's teachings are to be taken in their obvious sense, and are strictly true?

I answer, What is here taught as to prayer must be taken in connection with what is taught elsewhere. For example, what is here said of asking must be taken in connection with what is said of praying in faith—with what is said by James of asking and not receiving because men ask amiss, that they may consume it upon their lusts. If any of you were to frame a will or a promissory note, binding yourself or your administrators to pay over certain moneys, on certain specified conditions, you would not think it necessary to state the conditions more than once. Having stated them distinctly once, you would go on to state in detail the promise ; but you would not expect anybody to separate the promise from the condition, and then claim the promise without having fulfilled the condition, and even perhaps accuse you of falsehood because you did not fulfil the promise when the conditions had not been met.

Now, the fact is that we find, scattered throughout the Bible, various revealed conditions of prayer. Whoever would pray acceptably must surely fulfil not merely a part, but *all* of these conditions. Yet in practice, the church, to a great extent, have overlooked, or at least have failed to meet these conditions. For example, they often pray for the Holy Spirit for selfish reasons. This is fearfully common. The real motives are selfish. Yet they come before God and urge their request often and long,—perhaps with great importunity; yet they are selfish in their very prayers, and God cannot hear. They are not in their inmost souls ready to do or to suffer all God's holy will. God calls some of his children through long seasons of extremest suffering, obviously as a means of purifying their hearts ; yet many pray for pure hearts, and for the Spirit to purify their hearts, who would rebel at once if God should answer their prayers by means of such a course of providence. Or God may see it necessary to crucify your love of reputation, and for this end may subject you to a course of trial which will blow your reputation to the winds of heaven. Are you ready to hail the blessings of a subdued, unselfish heart, even though it be given by means of such discipline ?

Often your motive in asking for the Spirit is merely personal comfort and consolation—as if you would live all your spiritual life on sweetmeats. Others ask for it really as a matter of self-glorification. They would like to have their names emblazoned in the papers. It would be so gratifying to be held up as a miracle of grace—as a most remarkable Christian. Alas, how many, in va-

rious forms of it, are only offering selfish prayers! Even
a minister might pray for the Holy Spirit from only sin-
ister motives.   He might wish to have it said that he is
very spiritual, or a man of great spiritual power in his
preaching or his praying ; or he might wish to avoid that
hard study to which a man who has not the Spirit must
submit, since the Spirit does not teach him, nor give him
unction.   He might almost wish to be inspired, so easy
would this gift make his preaching and his study.   He
might suppose that he really longed to be filled with the
Spirit, while really he is only asking amiss, to consume
it on some unhallowed desire.   A student may pray for
the Spirit to help him study, and yet only his ambition
or his indolence may have inspired that prayer.   Let it
never be forgotten, we must sympathise with God's reasons for our having the Spirit, as we would hope to pray
acceptably.   There is nothing mysterious about this
matter.   The great end of all God's spiritual adminis-
trations towards us in providence or grace is to divest
us of selfishness, and to bring our hearts into harmony
with his in the spirit of real love.

Persons often quench the Spirit even while they are
praying for it.   One prays for the Spirit, yet that very
moment fails to notice the Spirit's monitions in his own
breast, or refuses to do what the Spirit would lead and
press him to do.   Perhaps they even pray for the Spirit,
that this gift may be a substitute for some self-denying
duty to which the Spirit has long been urging them.
This is no uncommon experience.   Such persons will
be very likely to think it very difficult to get the Spirit.
A woman was going to a female prayer-meeting, and

thought she wanted the Holy Spirit, and would make that her special errand at that meeting. Yet when there, the Spirit pressed her to pray audibly and she resisted, and excused herself.

It is common for persons to resist the Spirit in the very steps he chooses to take. They would make the Spirit yield to them; he would have them yield to him. They think only of having their blessings come in the way of their own choosing; he is wiser and will do it in his own way or not at all. If they cannot accept of his way, there can be no agreement. Often when persons pray for the Spirit, they have in their minds certain things which they would dictate to him as to the manner and circumstances. Such ought to know that if they would have the Spirit, they must accept him in his own way. Let him lead, and consider that your business is to follow. Thus it not unfrequently happens that professed Christians maintain a perpetual resistance against the Holy Spirit, even while they are ostensibly praying for his presence and power. When he would fain draw them, they are thinking of dictating to him, and refuse to be led by him in his way. When they come really to understand what is implied in being filled with the Spirit, they draw back. It is more and different from what they had thought. *That* is not what they wanted.

There is no difficulty in our obtaining the Holy Spirit if we are willing to have it; but this implies a willingness to surrender ourselves to his direction and discretion.